BORUCH LEARNS HIS BROCHOS

By Rabbi Shmuel Kunda

Graphics and color work by Yaffa Eichler

BORUCH LEARNS HIS BROCHOS

Written and illustrated by Rabbi Shmuel Kunda

This book is based on the tape *Boruch Learns His Brochos*, the first in the "Boruch Learns" story tape series, which also includes cassette tapes entitled *Boruch Learns About Shabbos, Boruch Makes A Simcha*, and *Boruch Learns About Pesach*.

I would like to express my special gratitude to my mother, wife, children and grandchildren, תחי׳, whose support made this and all my projects possible.

A Shevach V'hodoa to Hakadosh Baruch Hu for the zechus of working on Chinuch projects for Jewish children.

Special thanks to Rabbi Aaron Kunda for his guidance in color application.

First Cassette Production–1982
First Printed Edition–December 2005
Second Printing–July 2007
ISBN 978-1-932443-41-7

"Boruch Learns His Brochos"

© Copyright 2005, by Shmuel Kunda, 1560 51st St., Brooklyn, NY 11219   718-871-0521

All rights reserved.

No part of this publication may be translated, reproduced, stored in a retrieval system or transmitted, in any form or by any means, electronic, mechanical, photocopying, recording or otherwise, without prior permission in writing from Rabbi Shmuel Kunda.

THE RIGHTS OF THE COPYRIGHT HOLDER WILL BE STRICTLY ENFORCED.

Written by Rabbi Shmuel Kunda
Illustrated by Rabbi Shmuel Kunda
Book Design: Yaffa Eichler
Cover Design: Yaffa Eichler

A list of all Shmuel Kunda Productions can be found at the end of this book.

This illustrated story book corresponds to the original audio production, *Boruch Learns His Brochos*. Some words and lines have been changed and/or omitted to accommodate the written story. How many changes can you find? Send your answers to Rabbi Kunda.

Printed in China

"Hello, everybody. Oh, what a great day!
Not too hot, not too cold, it's just okay.
My mother packed me a picnic lunch
With lots of delicious food to munch!"

"Uh oh, I'm looking and searching,
But I don't see any bread.
Now a different *brocho* for each food must be said.
Cookies and candies and soda with bubbles.
Oy vey, do I have troubles!
I'll never know which *brochos* go
On all these fruits. Where do they grow?"

"Say, what's that across the street I see?
A store with a sign going up: Tzvi's Grocery.
I have an idea, a great inspiration!
That's where I'll get my correct information.
Yes, sir, that's where I'll go, sir.
I'll ask Tzvi the grocer!"

"Oh, come in, come in, we're open."

"That's what I was hopin'."

"Come in all the way. Don't be shy.
We've got lots of food for you to buy."

"Well, Mister Tzvi, it's like this, you see.
I kind of had a hunch,
As I was about to munch my lunch,
That since you're a grocer,
You would know, sir,
All the *brochos* and how they go, sir."

"Oh, look! It says, 'Section of *Borei Pri Ha-eitz.*'"

"Of course, Boruch, and if you really want to learn something, You should hear the way these fruit sing."

"Fruit that sing? I've never heard of that before."

"I told you that this is no ordinary grocery store."

Red cherries, blueberries,
Oranges they pack in crates,
Plums and peaches,
The seforim teach us
Are all *Ha-eitz*.

"Thank you, thank you, my friend, may you be blessed.
Rolling me over was really a *chessed*.
As you can see, *Hashem* did form us
To be so round and enormous."

"It's a good thing we grow out of the dirt,
'Cause for any tree growing watermelons,
Boy, would that hurt!
So, let me teach you a thing or three.
There's no such thing as a watermelon tree!"

"There's no such thing as a watermelon tree.
There never was and there never will be.
And I say nope, there is no hope,
Of a tree that grows a cantaloupe.
Or, if a tree grew honeydew
And the wind blew, it could land on you!
They're safe and sound growing on the ground,
So *Borei Pri Ho'adoma* for them is found."

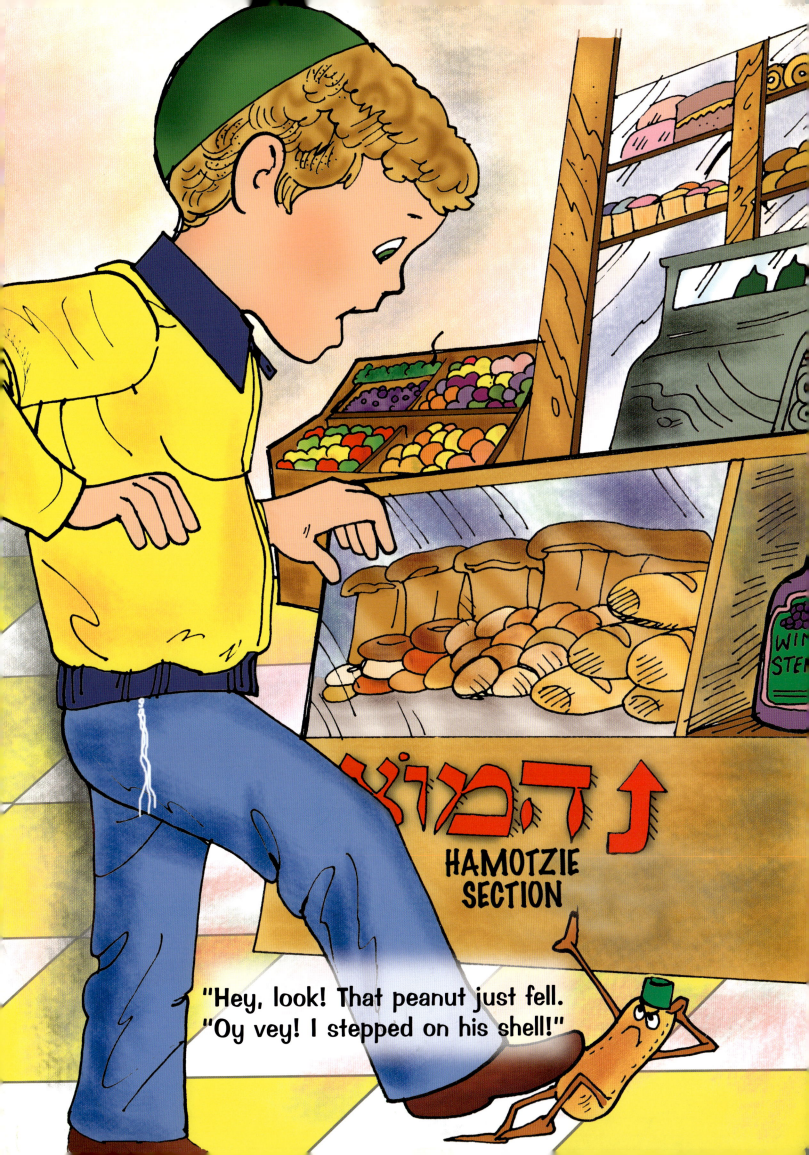

"Listen, the whole world sings
About the peanut's wonderful things!"

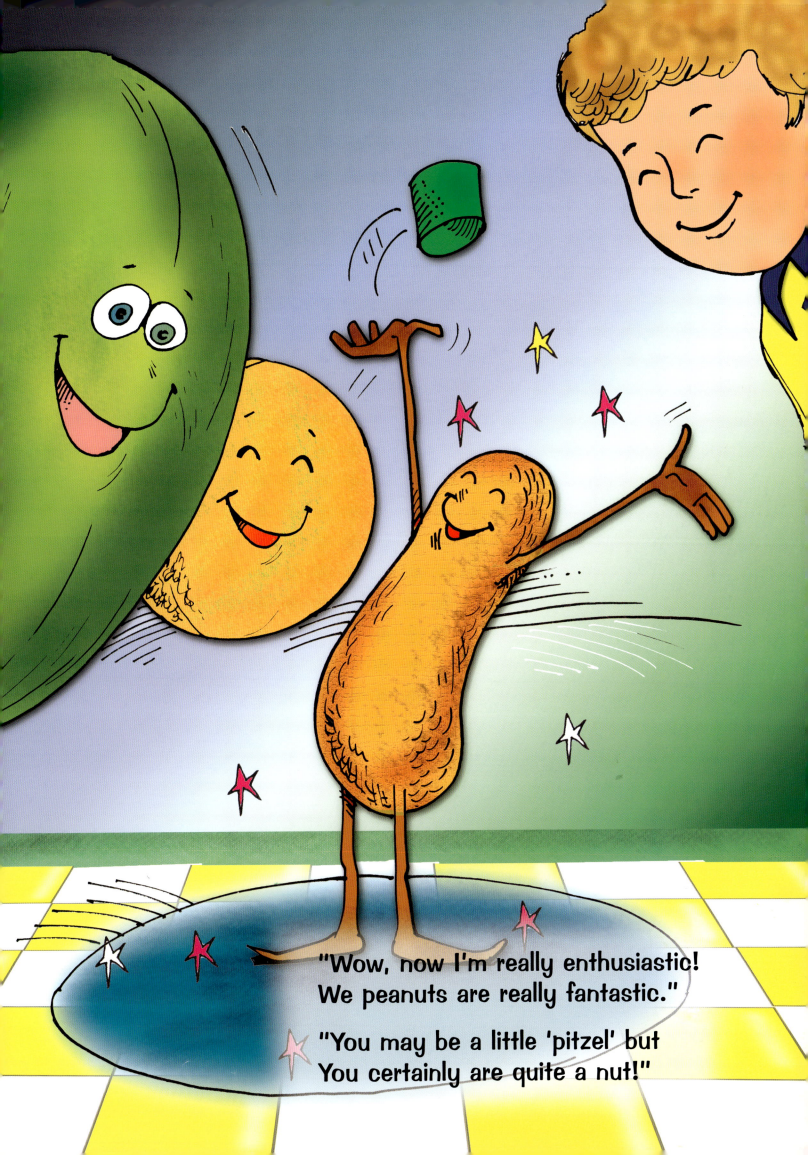

"We just came from very hot weather
Where we all hung on a tree together."

"On a TREE?!
So why on bananas is
Borei Pri Ho-adoma said?
Shouldn't it be *Ha-eitz* instead?"

"The banana tree doesn't stay
From year to year.
It just dries up and disappears.
So *Ho-adoma* is the one that's right
On bananas to recite."

"On every continent,
Each food is different.
In color, in taste and name,
No two are quite the same.
Hashem did this wondrous thing
To make life more interesting."

"The taste and smell are easy to tell.
That's what makes the food so inviting.
And when they're ripe,
Each one's a different type.
It makes the world so exciting!"

שֶׁהַכֹּל נִהְיָה בִּדְבָרוֹ

I love chocolate candy.
Jelly beans are handy,
And taffy that you chew so slow.
Sugar is sweet and sandy,
Ices so cool and dandy.
All are *She-hakol Ni-hiye Bidvoro!*

"Out of my way!
Stay clear!
I've got a big delivery here!"
It's me, Slippery Jake,
And I'm carrying a six-foot birthday cake!"

"Be careful, Jake. Just put down that cake
Near the cookies and things that you bake,
Very close
To the section of *Borei Minei Mezonos.*"

"Jake, Jake, for goodness sake,
Are you hurt anywhere, did anything break?"

"Ooh, ah! What a riot, what a scream!
I'm completely covered in frosting and cream!

"Well, at least you can learn the *bracha*
That you make
When you take a bite of a piece of cake."

"Oh, hello Barry, this is Mrs. Geffen on the line.
Could you please send over nine bottles of wine?
It's this little boy of mine.
His Bar Mitzvah is this Shabbos,
And Rabbi Klein
Said that at the Kiddush
We should have wine.
He said it's very Yiddish
To have wine at a Kiddush."

"My name is *Boruch*, and nine bottles of wine will be fine."

"Boruch, take a look!
Here comes my old friend Mr. Gazook,
The world famous chef, and baker, and cook.
His face looks full of worry!
He seems to be in an awful hurry."

"*Yom Tov* or *Shabbos*, or even a wedding...
There should be bread for *Hamotzie* at every setting.
Don't you worry, Mr. Gazook. Today you are in luck,
Because Slippery Jake just delivered bread and *challah* in his truck.
Just take as much as you need."

"Oy, you're a *tzadik*, ah Yeed!"

The Best Jewish Family Entertainment Ever

Shmuel Kunda
Classic Story Cassettes/CDs

Story Cassettes & CDs

- Boruch Learns his Brochos
- ברוך לומד את הברכות Hebrew version
- Boruch Learns about Shabbos
- Boruch Makes a Simcha
- Boruch Learns about Pesach
- The Incredible Dreidel of Feitel Von Zeidel
- The Magic Yarmulka
- The Longest Pesach
- The Talking Coins
- When Zaidy Was Young Tale 1
- When Zaidy Was Young Tale 2
- The Miraculous Menorah
- The Royal Rescue
- A Ton Of Mon
- Papa And The Prince
- Zaidy's Great Idea
- The Daring Disguise
- Where's Zaidy?
- There's Zaidy!

Books

- Boruch Learns his Brochos
- Boruch Learns about Pesach
- Chanuka Shpiel
- Pesach Shpiel
- Summer Shpiel
- Big Shpiel